SIMPLY ROMANTIC PIANO

Compiled and edited
by Joseph Smith

THE STEINWAY LIBRARY OF PIANO MUSIC

To Margaret Willard,
who inspired me to take up the piano.

— Joseph Smith

The Steinway Library of Piano Music is published by
Ekay Music Inc., Bedford Hills, New York 10507

Editor-in-chief: Edward Shanaphy
Project Coordinator: Stuart Isacoff
Designed by Luke Daigle/Daigle Interactive LLC
Production by Anita Tumminelli

Distributed by Warner Bros. Publications, Inc.
and Ekay Music Inc.

We would like to thank the Music Division of the New
York Public Library for the Performing Arts and the Sibley
Library of the Eastman School of Music for their help.

www.musicbooksnow.com

CONTENTS

A NOTE ABOUT 'LAY-FLAT' BINDING

This special binding is designed to keep your music book open on the music stand. It will need a slight preparation on your part to help it accomplish this. Place the book on a clean, flat surface and open it to a section near the front. With the heel of your hand, apply a gentle but firm pressure at various spots along the spine where the pages meet. Do not strike at the spine, and do not run your hand or thumb along the spine. This could cause the pages to wrinkle. Repeat this pressing process at various places throughout the book to break it in. When you have selected a piece to play, repeat the process again for that piece, and you may also, at this point, fold the book back on itself gently squeezing the binding.

INTRODUCTION

The short piano piece was particularly congenial to composers and audiences of the romantic era, uniting the succinctness of song with the ambiguity of "absolute" music. And, happily, many of these pieces are not difficult. Some are easy movements from concert cycles, some are from opuses probably intended for the home pianist, and some are from didactic works. But all embody a single vivid mood, or poetic idea.

This anthology is intended to be a practical, not a scholarly "urtext," edition. Nevertheless, I have made every effort to present the material in purest form. Each piece appears as the composer intended: complete, in its original key, with nothing changed or omitted. I have taken the pieces from the most authentic sources I could find—never from earlier anthologies that might have offered transcriptions or spurious works under the guise of original compositions.

I have offered many suggestions for redistributing material between the hands, in the interest of physical comfort: all are in the form of brackets. The player should of course only employ these if they prove to facilitate the passage. (In such cases, there may be a tradeoff: the redistribution will probably be easier to execute, but may require more mental effort to learn.) All fingering is mine. I am acutely aware that individuals differ in their preferences in this regard, but I hope that my fingerings will be helpful to some players—others may ignore them. My fingerings generally presuppose pedaling, even where pedaling is not marked.

I have treated pedal markings with apparent inconsistency—some pieces have many, some none, and some a few scattered markings. My principle has been to avoid cluttering the page with markings where the pedaling is obvious, but to supply pedalings where it seemed to me that some players might find them useful. I have tried to preserve any authorial pedalings, but occasionally modified them for the modern piano. Of course, romantic music usually demands a constant use of the pedal. It goes without saying that those with smaller hands will need to arpeggiate certain chords (for example, in the Burleigh piece) even where no arpeggiation is marked. Very occasionally, I have added marks of expression: for instance, I have supplied phrase marks to the Schubert A minor waltz, and amplified the dynamics of the Saumell piece.

A few of the pieces have key signatures with four or five accidentals. I hope this will not be discouraging—such keys may be more difficult for some players to read, but that in no way means that the pieces, once learned, are more difficult to play!

THE
MUSIC

EVENING PRAYER

from Twenty-Five Preludes, Op. 31

Charles Valentin Alkan ~ (1813–1888)

THE RETURNING HUNTER

from Eskimos, Op. 64

Amy Marcy Cheney Beach ~ (1867–1944)

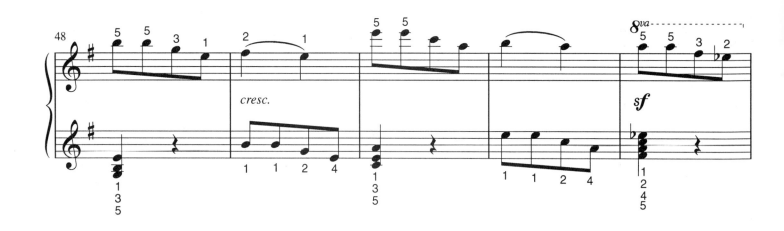

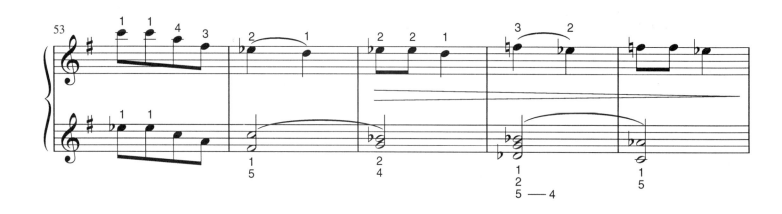

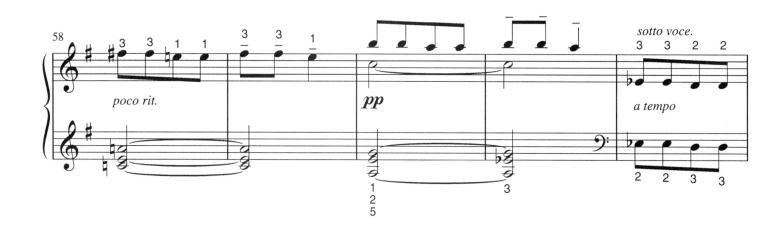

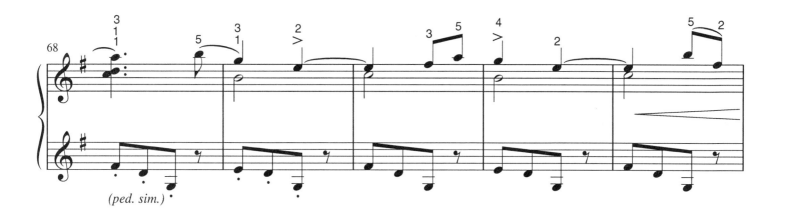

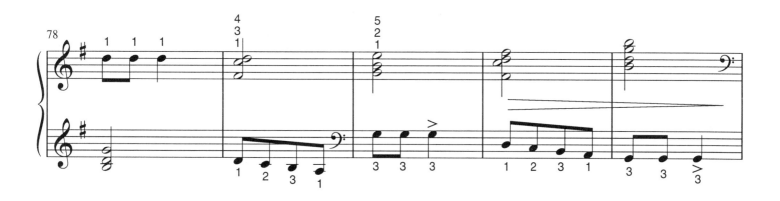

REVERIE

from Petite Suite

Alexander Borodin ~ (1833–1887)

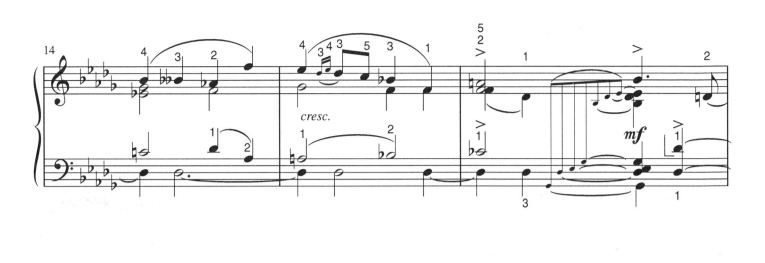

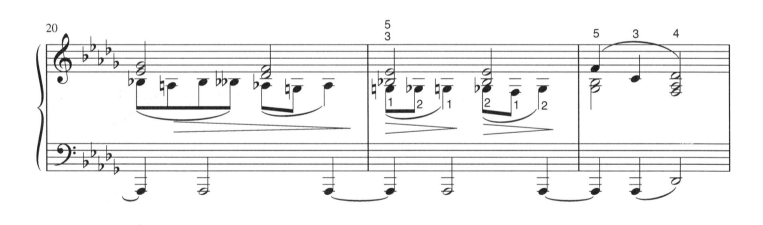

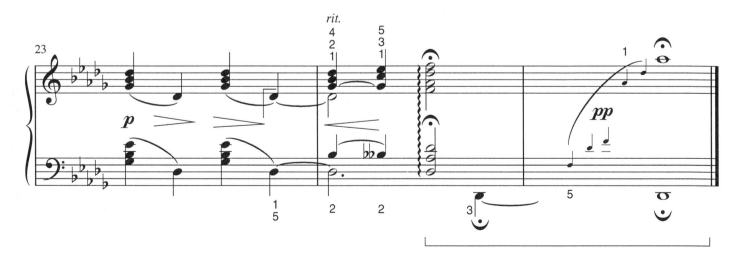

WALTZ IN D
WoO 85

Ludwig van Beethoven ~ (1770–1827)

HARMONY OF THE ANGELS

from Twenty-Five Easy and Progressive Studies, Op. 100

Friedrich Burgmüller ~ (1806–1874)

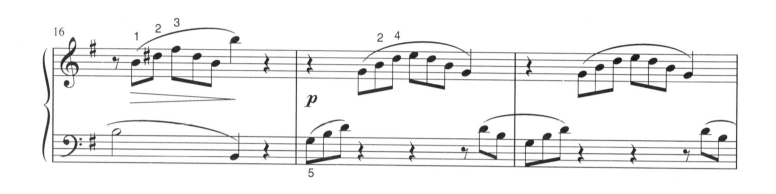

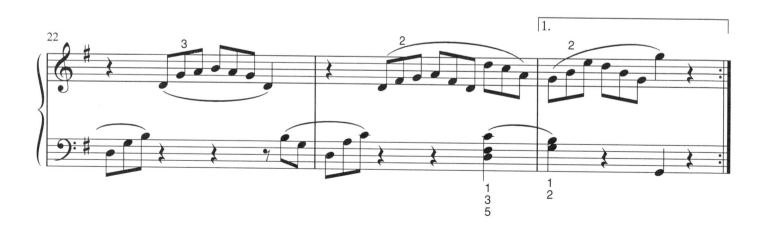

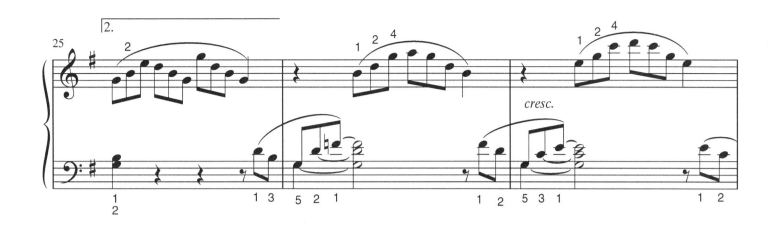

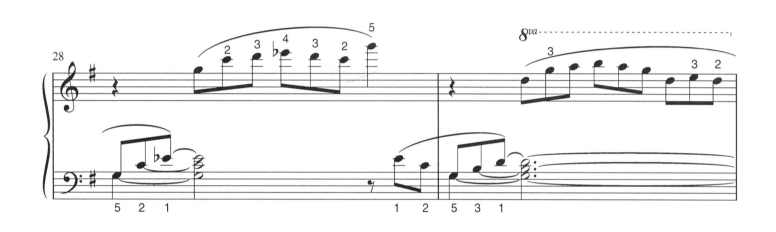

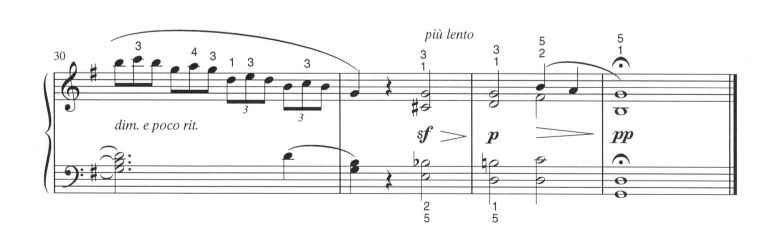

THROUGH MOANIN' PINES

from Piano Sketches: From the Southland

H. T. Burleigh ~ (1866–1949)

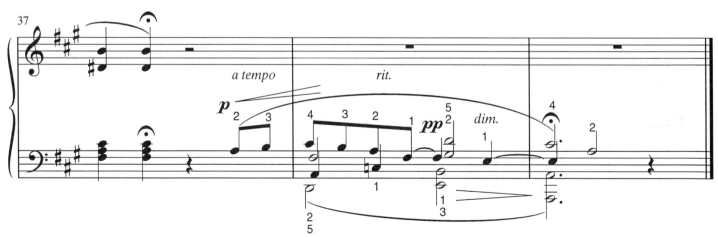

CANTABILE

Frédéric Chopin ~ (1810–1849)

THE TROUBADOUR

Nocturne in C

John Field ~ (1782–1837)

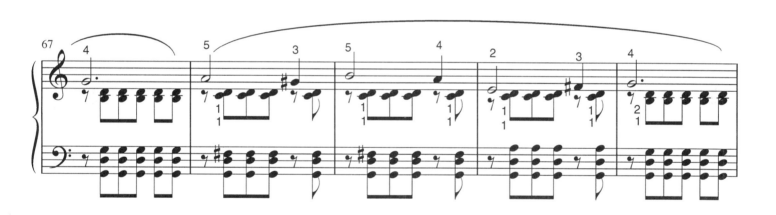

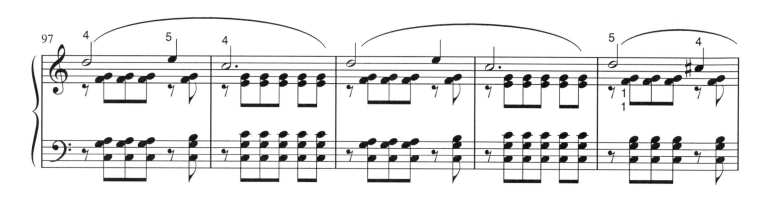

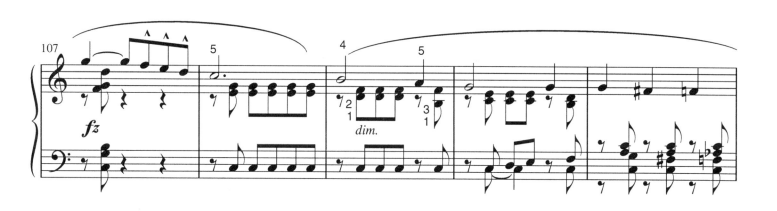

PRELUDE IN C MINOR

John Field ~ (1782–1837)

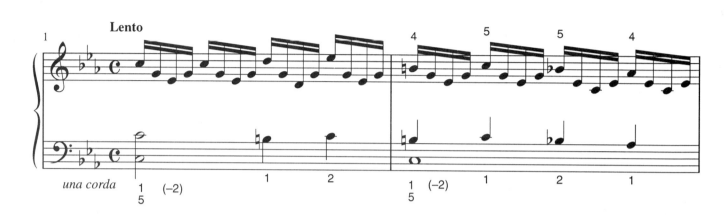

TARANTELLA

Mikhail Glinka ~ (1804–1857)

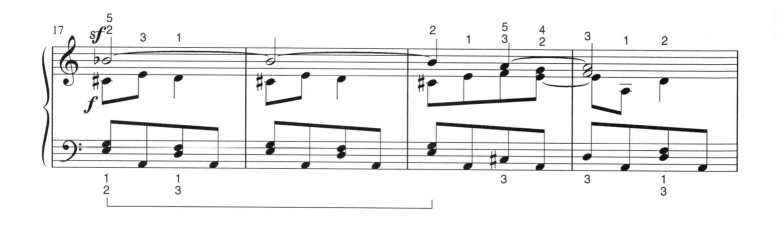

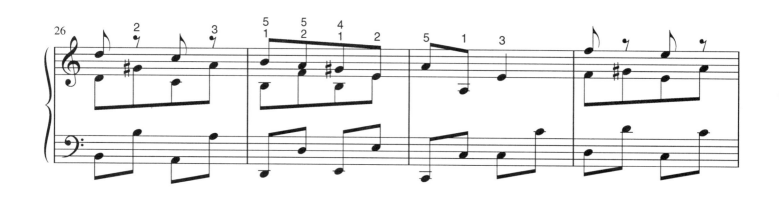

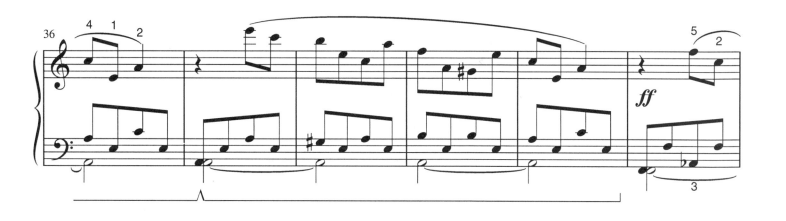

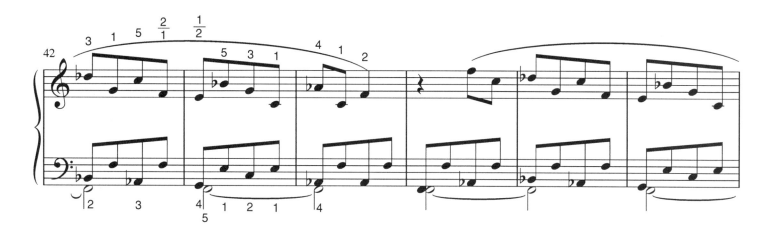

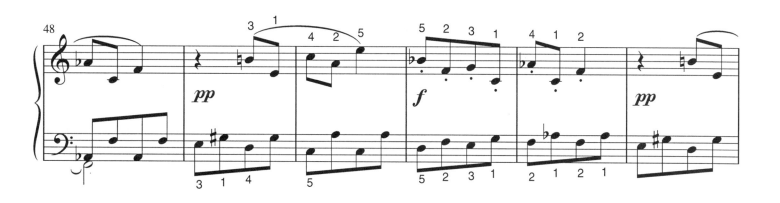

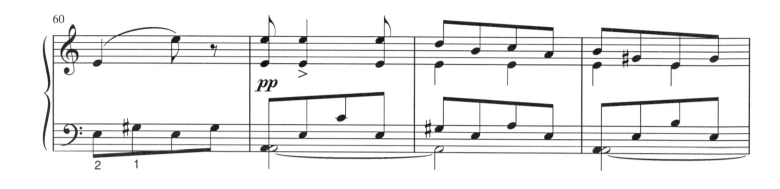

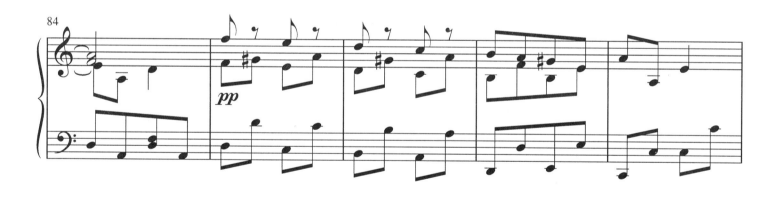

ALLEGRETTO
from Romantic Scenes

Enrique Granados ~ (1867–1916)

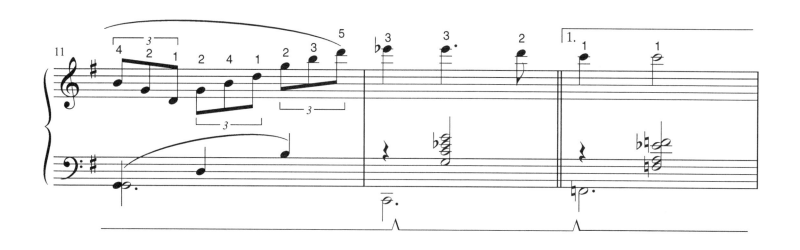

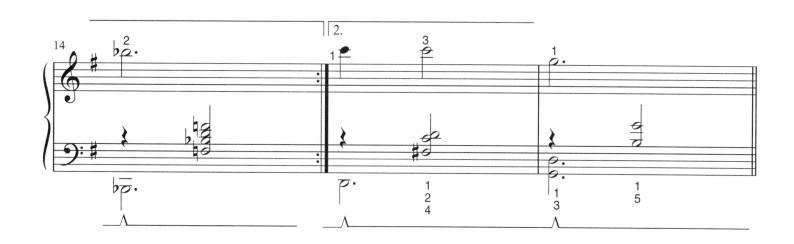

Andante

Small hands

OLD TALE

from Tales of Childhood, Op. 1

Enrique Granados ~ (1867–1916)

FOLKSONG

from Six Mountain Melodies

Edvard Grieg ~ (1843–1907)

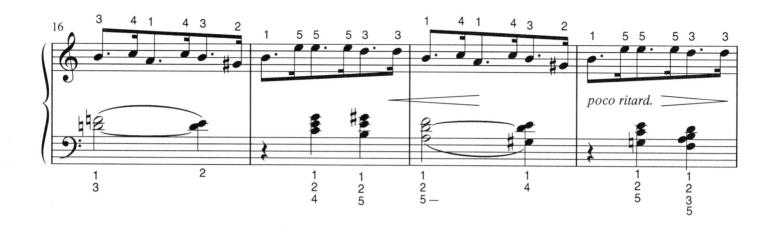

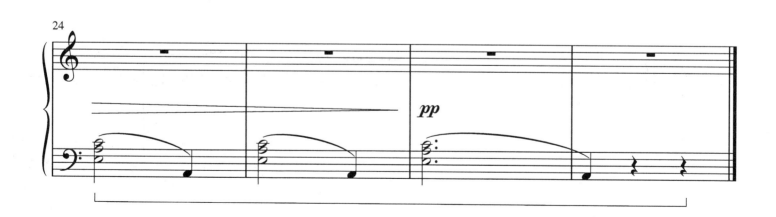

SAILOR'S SONG

from Lyric Pieces, Op. 68

Edvard Grieg ~ (1843–1907)

Allegro vivace e marcato

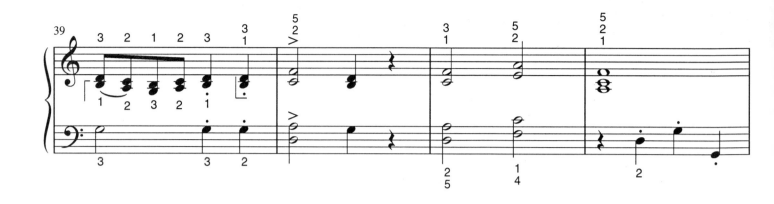

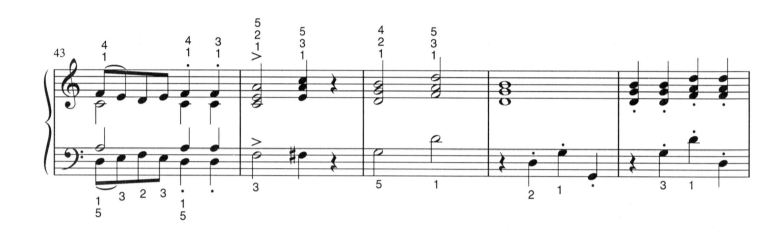

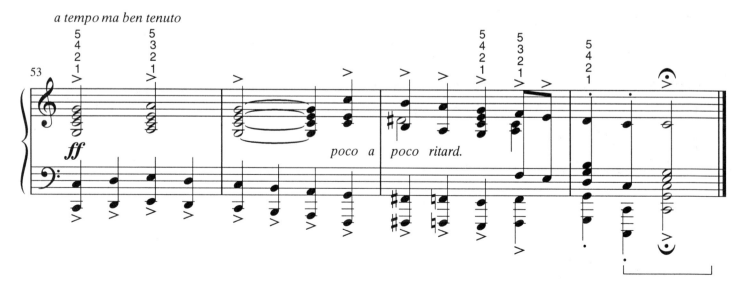

SPRINGDANCE

from Six Mountain Melodies

Edvard Grieg ~ (1843–1907)

PRELUDE
Op. 119, No. 28

Stephen Heller ~ (1814–1888)

Copyright ©2005 Ekay Music, Inc.

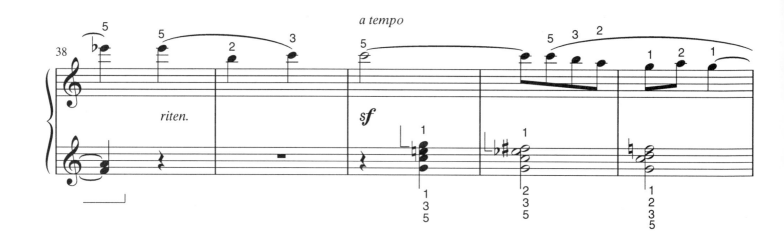

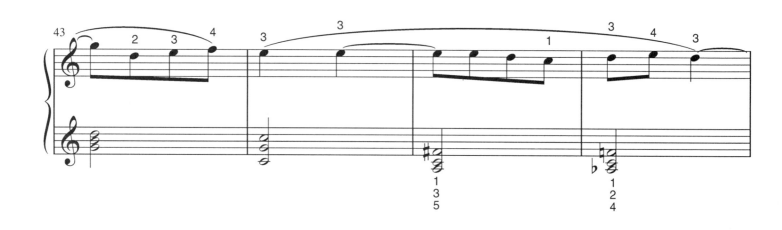

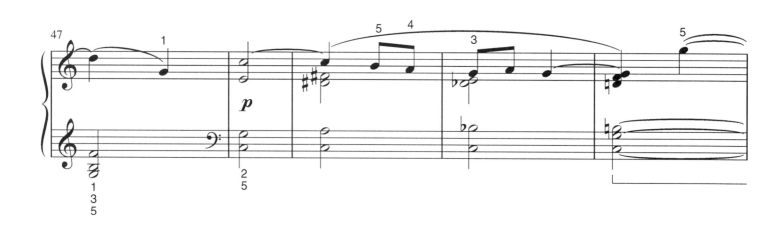

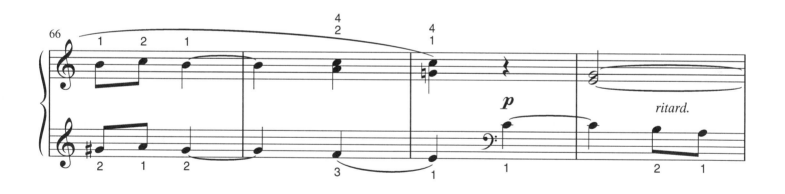

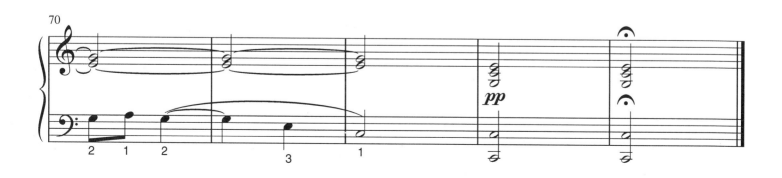

PIECE IN E
from Four Little Piano Pieces

Franz Liszt ~ (1811–1886)

Sehr langsam (Adagio)

ANDANTE SOSTENUTO

from Six Pieces for Children, Op. post. 72

Felix Mendelssohn ~ (1809–1847)

TO A WILD ROSE

from Woodland Sketches

Edward MacDowell ~ (1860–1908)

*Smaller hands can avoid the tenths thus:

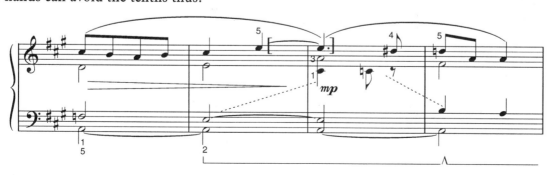

DRINK, TOMÁS!

¡¡Toma, Tomás!!–Cuban Contradanza

Manuel Saumell ~ (1817–1870)

The pulse of this piece fluctuates between 3/4 and 6/8.

SENTIMENTAL WALTZ

from Op. 50, D. 779

Franz Schubert ~ (1797–1828)

LANDLER

from D.366

Franz Schubert ~ (1797–1828)

LITTLE PIECE

from Album for the Young, Op. 68

Robert Schumann ~ (1810–1856)

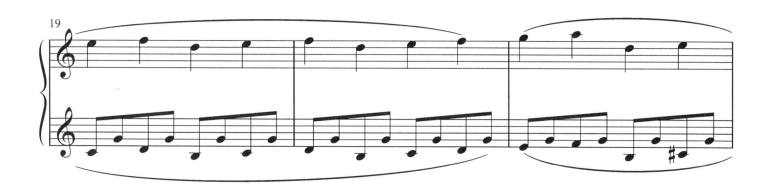

LITTLE LULLABY
from *Album Leaves, Op. 124*

Robert Schumann ~ *(1810–1856)*

NORTHERN SONG

from Album for the Young, Op. 68

Robert Schumann ~ *(1810–1856)*

PRELUDE IN A-FLAT

Op. 11, No. 17

Alexander Scriabin ~ *(1872–1915)*

SWEET REVERIE

from Album for the Young

Peter Ilyitch Tchaikovsky ~ (1840–1893)

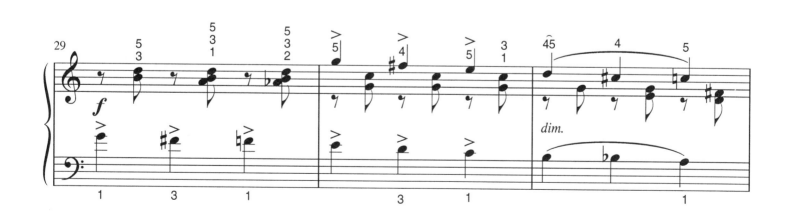

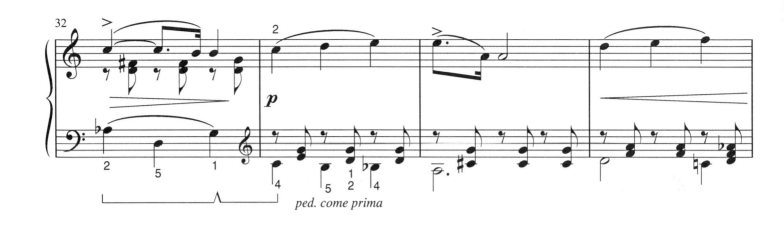

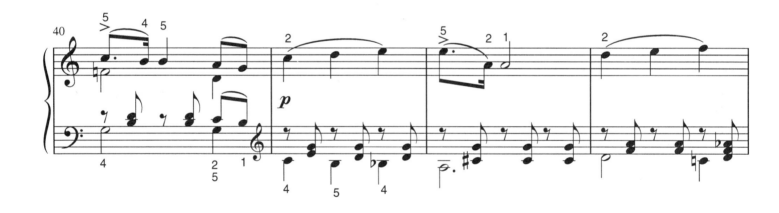

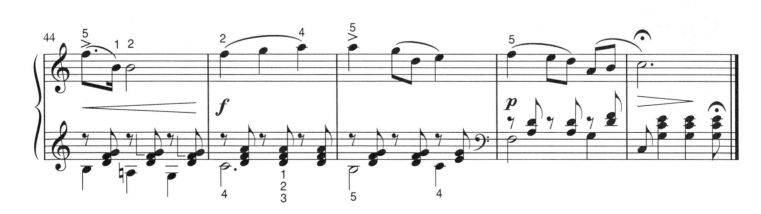

KAMARINSKAYA

Russian Folk Dance, from Album for the Young

Peter Ilyitch Tchaikovsky ~ (1840–1893)

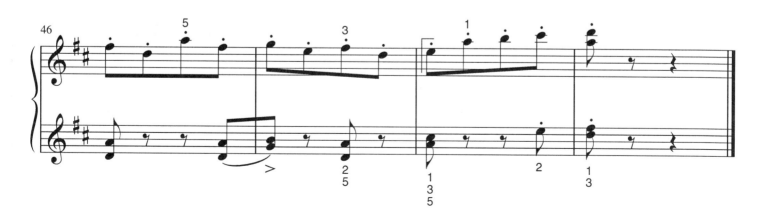

LULLABY

Hugo Wolf ~ (1860–1903)

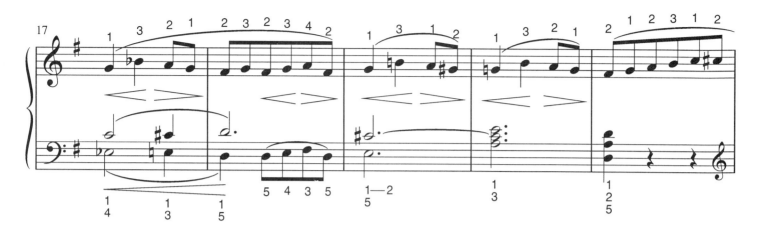

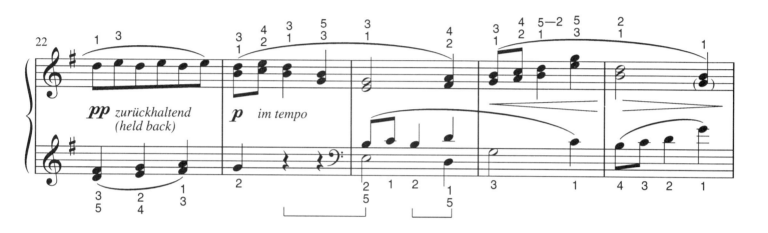

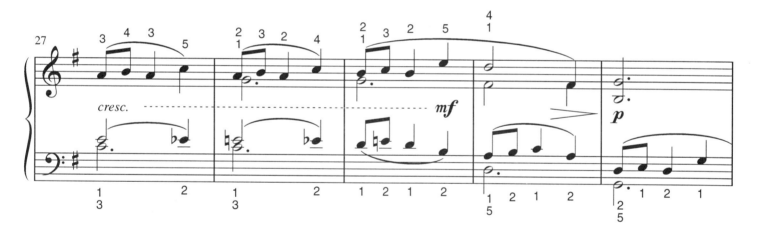

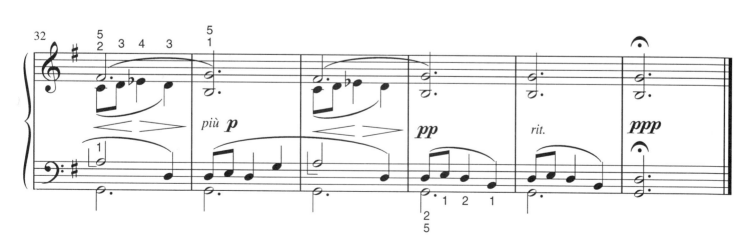

DOLCE

Johann Strauss, Jr. ~ *(1825-1899)*

This is a strain which appears in Strauss's *Adele Waltzes*, written out by him in piano score as a musical autograph.